Many Hearts
Beating as One

Other books by Marilyn R. Moody

Courage & Cancer
A Breast Cancer Diary
A Journey from Cancer to Cure

Breast Cancer Sisters

Love & Laughter
The True Story of an
Online Cancer Survivors' Support Group

Love, Fear & Other Things that Cry Out in the Night
Moments Alone with Agoraphobia

Simple Pleasures
A Love Letter to My Grandchildren

Hummingbird Wings, Friendship & Other Things
A Book of Sonoma Memories

The Moody's and Coffin's and Everyone
One Family's Tales and Genealogy

Many Hearts Beating as One

Some Favorite Inspirational Quotes

Compiled by

Marilyn R. Moody

To order additional copies of this book, contact:
Xlibris Corporation
1-888-795-4274
www.Xlibris.com
Orders@Xlibris.com
57407

And, who do I thank?

Obviously these famous,
and not so famous,
people from the past and
the present who have
expressed themselves in such a way
that gives me much pleasure and hope.

Dedicated to
all those wise people who
have such a way with words,
and also to those
who pass on their words.

All truly wise thoughts have been thought already,
thousands of times; but to make them truly ours,
we must think them over again honestly,
until they take firm root in our personal experience.

Johann Wolfgang von Goethe

Introduction

I have this thing that I'm sure I share with many others. It is that of enjoying a really good and inspirational quote. Over the years I've bought books of them, clipped them from magazines and newspapers and of course in more recent years, borrowed them from the internet. I kept a list of them and finally decided I wanted them for myself in one place, somewhere that would be easily accessible to get to when needed. That's what began the compiling of these bits and pieces from over the years.

I've taken others' words as to who to give the credit to, but once—when I saw that I had the same quote by two different people—I realized some quotes might not be from those claimed to be the originator. Please forgive any errors in the quotes, or who I have listed as its author, but do go ahead and enjoy them as I have and still do.

Marilyn R. Moody
December 2008
Cypress, CA

Start where you are.
Use what you have.
Do what you can.
It will be enough.

Unknown

Live as you will have wished
to have lived when you are dying.

Christian F. Gellert

Imagination was given to us to
compensate for what we are not;
a sense of humor was given to us to
console us for what we are.

Mark McGinnis

A journey of a thousand miles
must begin with a single step.

Chinese Proverb

You should not suffer the past.
You should be able to
wear it like a loose garment.

Take it off and let it drop.

Eva Jessye

People rarely succeed
unless they have fun
in what they are doing.

Dale Carnegie

Courage isn't the absence of fear.
Courage is taking action
in the face of fear.

Mark Twain

You don't drown by falling into the water.
You drown by staying there.

Katherine Hepburn

Be patient with your enemies,
and forgiving of your friends.

Afghan Proverb

Every artist dips his brush into his own soul,
and paints his own nature into his pictures.

Henry Ward Beecher

Whenever you do a thing,
act as if all the world were watching.

Thomas Jefferson

We must all suffer one of two things:
the pain of discipline or
the pain of regret or disappointment.

Jim Rohn

Being passionate about something
is the key to success.

But using that passion to help others
is the key to happiness

Arnold Schwarzenegger

Time is the stuff
that life is made of.

Benjamin Franklin

Correction does much,
but encouragement does more.

Johann Wolfgang von Geothe

Accept challenges so that
you may feel
the exhilaration of victory.

George S. Patton

It takes as much stress
to be a success
as it does to be a failure.

Emilio James Trujillo

Things work out best for those
who make the best
of the way things work out.

Abraham Lincoln

We live very close together.
So, our prime purpose in this life
is to help others.

And if you can't help them,
at least don't hurt them.

Dalai Lama

We cannot truly face life
until we face the fact
that it will be taken away from us.

Billy Graham

Death is not the greatest loss in life.
The greatest loss is
what dies within us
while we live.

Norman Cousins

Wherever you go,
go with all your heart.

Confucius

The only way to have a friend
is to be one.

Ralph Waldo Emerson

Kindness makes a fellow feel good,
whether it's being done to him or by him.

Frank A. Clark

There is joy in work.
There is no happiness except in the realization
that we have accomplished something.

Henry Ford

Never seem more learned
than the people you are with.
Wear your learning like a pocket watch
and keep it hidden.
Do not pull it out to count the hours,
but give the time when you are asked.

Lord Chesterfield

A happy person is not a person
in a certain set of circumstances,
but rather a person with
a certain set of attitudes.

Hugh Downs

One important key to success is self-confidence.
An important key to self-confidence is preparation.

Arthur Ashe

Remember you don't have to get it perfect . . .
just get it going.

Alexandria Brown

Often God has to shut a door in our face
so that He can subsequently
open the door
through which He wants us to go.

Catherine Marshall

It's a funny thing about life;
if you refuse to accept anything but the best,
you very often get it.

Somerset Maugham

A good laugh and a long sleep
are the best cures in the doctor's book.

Irish Proverb

The experience of others adds to our knowledge,
but not to our wisdom; that is dearer bought.

Hosea Ballou

&

A man should look for what is,
and not for what he thinks should be.

Albert Einstein

There can be no happiness if the things we believe in
are different from the things we do.

Freya Stark

Time you enjoyed wasting,
is not time wasted.

T.S. Eliot

Think left and think right
and think low and think high.
Oh, the thinks you can think up
if only you try.

Dr. Seuss

Tell me your friends,
and I'll tell you who you are.

Assyrian Proverb

Happiness depends upon ourselves.

Aristotle

B

Since you get more joy
out of giving joy to others,
you should put a good deal of thought
into the happiness you are able to give.

Eleanor Roosevelt

Happiness is not a destination.
It is a method of life.

Burton Hills

When will you know you have enough,
and what will you do then?

Barbara De Angelis

There cannot be a crisis next week.
My schedule is already full.

Henry Kissinger

The way I see it,
if you want the rainbow
you gotta put up with the rain.

Dolly Parton

Every man goes down to his death
bearing in his hands
only that which
he has given away.

Persian Proverb

If someone can't treat you right,
love you back and see your worth,
let it go.

T. D. Jakes

Keep your eyes wide open
before marriage,
and half shut afterwards.

Benjamin Franklin

Do not follow where the path may lead.
Go instead where there is
no path and leave a trail.

Harold McAlindon

When you develop yourself to the point
where your belief in yourself is so strong
that you know you can
accomplish anything you
put your mind to—
your future will be unlimited.

Brian Tracy

I'm a great believer in luck,
and I find the harder I work,
the more luck I have.

Thomas Jefferson

The miracle is this—
the more we share,
the more we have.

Leonard Nimoy

It takes courage to grow up and
turn out to be who you really are.

ee cummings

Character cannot be developed
in ease and quiet.
Only through experience of trial
and suffering
can the soul be strengthened,
ambition inspired,
and success achieved.

Helen Keller

He knows the water best
who has waded through it.

Danish Proverb

One of the things I keep learning
is that the secret of being happy
is doing things for other people.

Dick Gregory

It's never too late to be
what you might have been.

George Elliot

Love is blind;
friendship closes its eyes.

Anonymous

One who knows how to show
and to accept kindness
will be a friend better
than any possession.

Sophocles

That best portion of a good man's life—
his little, nameless, unremembered
acts of kindness and of love.

William Wordsworth

If you would be loved,
love and be lovable.

Benjamin Franklin

Happiness is never stopping to think
if you are.

Palmer Sondreal

Develop an attitude
of gratitude,
and give thanks for everything
that happens to you,
knowing that every step forward
is a step toward achieving
something bigger and better than
your current situation.

Brian Tracy

You can never be happy at the expense
of the happiness of others.

Chinese Proverb

Don't let yourself forget
what it's like to be sixteen.

Anonymous

The best way to cheer yourself up
is to try to cheer somebody else up.

Mark Twain

No one is useless in this world
who lightens the burden
of it for anyone else.

Charles Dickens

You live more fully
once you realize
that any time spent
being unhappy
is wasted.

Ruth E. Renkel

Most folks are about as happy
as they make up their minds to be.

Abraham Lincoln

An insincere and evil friend
is more to be feared than a wild beast;
a wild beast may wound your body,
but an evil friend will wound your mind.

Buddha

A very important part of the joy of living
is the joy of giving.

William Buck

There is only one way to happiness and
that is to cease worrying about things,
which are beyond the power
of our will.

Epictetus

Efficiency is intelligent laziness.

Anonymous

Speak little,
do much.

Benjamin Franklin

The true way to soften one's troubles
is to solace those of others.

Madame De Maintenon

If you want to make
good use of your time,
you've got to know
what's most important
and then give it all you've got.

Lee Iacocca

Things turn out best
for the people
who make the best
of the way things turn out.

John Wooden

The purpose of life is not
to be happy but to matter,
to be productive, to be useful,
to have it make some difference
that you have lived at all.

Leo Rosten

The time to make friends
is before you need them.

Traditional Proverb

If you would know the road ahead,
ask someone who has traveled it.

Chinese Proverb

Every little blessing
is far too precious to ever forget
to say "thank you."

Laura Regis

May you live all the days of your life.

Jonathan Swift

Life is not easy for any of us.

Marie Curie

People become really quite remarkable when
they start thinking that they can do things.

When they believe in themselves
they have the first secret of success.

Norman Vincent Peale

Take the first step in faith.
You don't have to see
the whole staircase,
just take the first step.

Martin Luther King, Jr.

If you really want something,
you can figure out how to make it happen.

Cher

Better to light
one small candle
than to curse the darkness.

Chinese Proverb

Success is the sum of small efforts,
repeated day in and day out.

Robert Collier

The best and most beautiful things
in this world cannot be seen
or even heard, but must be felt
with the heart.

Helen Keller

Happiness is not having what you want,
but wanting what you have.

Anonymous

You gain strength,
courage, and confidence
by every experience in which you
really stop to look fear in the face.
You must do the thing,
which you think you cannot do.

Eleanor Roosevelt

The best way to find yourself,
is to lose yourself
in the service of others.

Ghandi

Every child is an artist.
The problem is to remain an artist
once he grows up.

Pablo Picasso

Courage is not the absence of fear,
but rather the judgment
that something else
is more important than fear.

Ambrose Redmoon

Keep steadily before you the fact
that all true success depends
at last upon yourself.

Theodore T. Hunger

One of the greatest
discoveries a man makes,
one of his great surprises,
is to find he can do
what he was afraid he couldn't do.

Henry Ford

Happiness is a choice
that requires effort at times.

Anonymous

No one became poor
by giving alms.

French Proverb

Hope is the feeling
you have that the feeling
you have isn't permanent.

Jean Kerr

Life's most persistent and urgent question is,
"What are you doing for others?"

Martin Luther King, Jr.

My religion is very simple.
My religion is kindness.

The Dalai Lama

The true measure of a person
is how they treat someone who
can do them absolutely no good.

Ann Landers

You can have everything in life you want
if you'll just help enough other people
to get what they want.

Zig Ziglar

I am thankful for laughter,
except when milk comes out of my nose.

Woody Allen

Prepare your mind to receive
the best that life has to offer.

Ernest Holmes

A coward gets scared and quits.
A hero gets scared, but still goes on.

Anonymous

You are what you think about all day long.

Robert Schuller

ℰ

Who you are speaks so loudly
I can't hear what you're saying.

Ralph Waldo Emerson

While one person hesitates
because he feels inferior,
the other is busy making mistakes
and becoming superior.

Henry C. Link

Be the change
you want to see in the world.

Ghandi

Kindness matters.
It is longed for and lived for.

Unknown

Find a need
and fill it.

Henry J. Kaiser

I've had some terrible times in my life,
some of which actually happened.

Mark Twain

ℬ

Live as if you were to die tomorrow;
learn as if you were to live forever.

Gandhi

You have not lived
until you have done something
for someone who can never repay you.

Anonymous

Choose a job you love,
and you will never have to work
a day in your life.

Confucius

One of the most remarkable compensations
of life is that no person can help another
without helping themselves.

Ralph Waldo Emerson

Rain and sunshine are to flowers
as praise is to the human spirit.

Unknown

Happiness is not a destination.
It is a method of life.

Burton Hills

Ω

They can because
they think they can.

Virgil

Happiness is
a state of activity.

Aristotle

Courage is
going from failure to failure
without losing enthusiasm.

Winston Churchill

The first step is to find out
what you love—
and don't be practical about it.

The second step is to
start doing what you love immediately,
in any small way possible.

Barbara Sher

Be gentle and you can be bold;
be frugal and you can be liberal;
avoid putting yourself before others and
you can become a leader among men.

Lao Tzu

R

The person who moves a mountain
begins by carrying away small stones.

Chinese Proverb

Our greatest glory is not in never falling,
but in rising every time we fall.

Confucius

There must be more to life
than having everything.

Maurice Sendak

The best motivation always comes
from within.

Michael Johnson

A world of abundance surrounds you,
if only you will step up and claim it.
Make life happen through you,
rather than letting it happen to you.

It will make all the difference in the world.

Ralph Marston

Do not wait for leaders—
do it alone,
person to person.

Mother Teresa

Most people can do extraordinary things
if they have the confidence or take the risks.

Yet most people don't.

They sit in front of the telly
and treat life as if it
goes on forever.

Philip Adams

When you're going through hell,
keep going.

Winston Churchill

When you carry out acts of kindness
you get a wonderful feeling inside.
It is as though something
inside your body responds
and says, yes,
this is how I ought to feel.

Rabbi Harold Kushner

We have committed
the Golden Rule to memory.
Now let us commit it to life.

Edwin Markham

The only gift
is a portion of thyself.

Ralph Waldo Emerson

Do what you love.
The money will follow.

 Marsha Sinetar

You must
motivate yourself
every day.

Matthew Stasior

I am beginning to learn that
it is the sweet, simple things of life,
which are the real ones after all.

Laura Ingalls Wilder

The art of being wise
is knowing what to overlook.

William James

You cannot do a kindness too soon,
for you never know
how soon it will be too late.

Ralph Waldo Emerson

What the mind dwells on,
expands.

Norman Vincent Peale

The truth of the matter is that
you always know the right thing to do.
The hard part is doing it.

H. Norman Schwarzkopf

A person's true wealth is
the good he or she does
in the world.

Mohammed

Life does not have to be perfect
to be wonderful.

Annette Funicello

Eighty percent of success is
showing up.

Woody Allen

Life is ours to be spent,
not to be saved.

D. H. Lawrence

A life isn't significant
except for its impact on other lives.

Jackie Robinson

The game of life
is the game of boomerangs.
Our thoughts,
words and deeds
return to us—sooner or later—
with astounding accuracy.

Florence Shinn

There is an intimate laughter
to be found
only among friends.

Maya Angelou

The unselfish effort
to bring cheer to others
will be the beginning
of a happier life
for ourselves.

Helen Keller

The more a man knows,
the more he forgives

Catherine the Great

ℐ

Problems are messages.

Shakti Gawai

Why aren't you happy?

It's because 99%
of everything you do,
and think,
and say,
is for yourself.

Wu Wei Wu

Do not wait
for extraordinary circumstances
to do good;
try using ordinary situations.

Jean Paul Richter

It is a happy talent
to know how to play.

Ralph Waldo Emerson

Work like you
don't need money.
Love like
you've never been hurt.
Sing as if
no one can hear you.
And dance like
no one's watching.

Unknown

ℬ

Only the wise and brave man
dares own he was wrong.

Benjamin Franklin

I believe that
one of the most important things to learn in life is
that you can make a difference in your community
no matter who you are, or where you live.
I have seen so many good deeds—
people helped, lives improved—
because someone cared.

Rosalynn Carter

The secret of getting ahead
is getting started.
The secret of getting started
is breaking your
complex overwhelming tasks
into small manageable tasks,
and then starting on the first one.

Mark Twain

A good deed is never lost.
He who sows courtesy
reaps friendship;
and he who plants kindness
gathers love.

Basil

A loving heart is
the truest wisdom.

Charles Dickens

Don't aim for success if you want it;
just do what you love and believe in,
and it will come naturally.

David Frost

The tragedy of life is not
that it ends so soon,
but that we wait so long to begin it.

Anonymous

Do the kinds of things that
come from the heart.
When you do,
you won't be dissatisfied,
you won't be envious,
you won't be longing for
somebody else's things.
On the contrary,
you'll be overwhelmed with
what comes back.

Morrie Schwartz

No one else, ever,
will think you're great
the way your mother does.

Mary Matalin

The richest person is the one
who is contented with what he has.

Robert C. Savage

The pessimist sees the difficulty
in every opportunity;
the optimist, sees the opportunity
in every difficulty.

L. P. Jacks

The sole meaning of life is
to serve humanity.

Leo Tolstoy

We cannot become what
we need to be
by remaining what we are.

Max DePree

Success seems to be
largely a matter of hanging on
after others have let go.

William Feather

Very few burdens are heavy
if everyone lifts.

Sy Wise

And when the broken hearted people—
living in the world agree,
there will be an answer—
"Let it be."

Paul McCartney

Before marriage,
a man will lie awake all night
thinking about something you said;
after marriage, he'll fall asleep
before you finish saying it.

Helen Rowland

Every life has its dark
and cheerful hours.
Happiness comes from choosing
which to remember.

Anonymous

We do not remember days.
We remember moments.

Cesare Pavese

And life is what we make it,
always has been,
always will be.

Grandma Moses

To be wronged
is nothing unless
you continue to remember it.

Confucius

Abundance is about being rich,
with or without money.

Suze Orman

Adversity causes some men to break,
others to break records.

William Arthur Ward

Riches come
not from an abundance of worldly goods,
but from a contented mind.

Mohammed

Close your eyes in fields of wonder.
Close your eyes and dream.
Close your eyes in fields of wonder.
Close your eyes and dream.

Van Morrison

If you look at what you have in life,
you'll always have more.
If you look at what you don't have in life,
you'll never have enough.

Oprah Winfrey

There is more hunger
for love and appreciation
in this world
than for bread.

Mother Teresa

Behave toward everyone
as if receiving a great guest.

Confucius

We cannot choose the things that
will happen to us.
But we can choose
the attitude we will take
toward anything that happens.

Success or failure depends on your attitude.

Alfred A. Montapert

Don't hurry, don't worry.
You're only here for a short visit.
So be sure to stop and smell the flowers.

Walter Hagen

Character cannot be developed
in ease and quiet.
Only through experience
of trial and suffering can
the soul be strengthened,
ambition inspired,
and success achieved.

Helen Keller

I expect to go through this world but once.
Therefore, if there be any good that
I can do or any kindness that I can show
to any fellow creature,
let me do it now,
for I shall not pass
this way again.

William Penn

Do not handicap your children
by making their lives easy.

Robert A. Heinlen

To change one's life:
Start immediately.
Do it flamboyantly.
No exceptions.

William James

Life is a series of experiences,
each one of which makes us bigger,
even though sometimes it is hard
to realize this.

Henry Ford

Running down people is a bad habit,
whether you are a gossip or a motorist.

Anonymous

If you do not learn to love and forgive others
everywhere you go,
you are going to suffer.

Eknath Easwaran

Live each day as if your life
had just begun.

Johann von Goethe

Some pursue happiness,
others create it.

Anonymous

Don't be afraid your life will end;
be afraid that it will never begin.

Grace Hansen

If you think you can do a thing
or think you can't do a thing,
you're right.

Henry Ford

As long as you're going to
think anyway,
think BIG.

Donald Trump

Dreams are extremely important.
You can't do it unless you imagine it.

George Lucas

If I'm ever stuck on a respirator
or a life-support system,
I definitely want to be unplugged—
but not till I get down to a size 8.

Henriette Mantel

Life is too complicated
not to be orderly.

Martha Stewart

Forgiveness is
having the courage to take down
the walls that we think
are there to protect us.

Suztes40

Every experience prepares you
for the next one.
You just don't ever know what
the next one is going to be.

Howard Schultz

We grow in time
to trust the future
for our answers.

Ruth Benedice

The more you get,
the more you've got to
take care of.

Alice Dormann

There can be no progress
unless people have faith
in tomorrow.

John F. Kennedy

Why not go out on a limb?
Isn't that where the fruit is?

Frank Scully

There is no happiness
in having or in getting,
but only in giving.

Henry Drummond

Finding a way to live the simple life today
is man's most complicated task.

Henry A. Courtney

The true measure of a man is how
he treats someone who
can do him absolutely no good.

Samuel Johnson

Appreciation makes people feel
more important than anything else
you can give them.

Unknown

We all live with the objective
of being happy;
our lives are all different
and yet the same.

Anne Frank

Love life,
engage in it,
give it all you've got.

Love it with passion,
because life truly does give back,
many times over what you put into it.

Maya Angelou

Sometimes in our lives
we all have pain,
we all have sorrow.
But, if we are wise
we know that there's
always tomorrow.

Bill Withers

Trouble is a part of life;
if you don't share it,
you don't give the person who loves you
a chance to love you enough.

Dinah Shore

Crises do not make friends—
they reveal them

Don Ward

Fashion your life
as a garland of beautiful deeds.

Buddha

We make a living
by what we get,
but we make a life
by what we give.

Henry Bucher

The beauty of the world around us is
only according to what we, ourselves,
bring to it.

Ralph Waldo Emerson

Happiness is not in
the mere possession of money;
it lies in the joy of achievement,
in the thrill of creative effort.

Franklin D. Roosevelt

Real charity doesn't care
if it's tax-deductible or not.

Dan Bennett

Killing time is not
a victimless crime.
Time for each of us is finite,
and when we kill time,
we also kill dreams,
opportunities,
maybe even life itself.

Anonymous

Your work is to
discover your work
and then with all your heart to
give yourself to it.

Buddha

Be what nature intended you for
and you will succeed.

Sydney Smith

There are only so many tomorrows.

Michael Landon

Small deeds done
are better than
great deeds planned.

Peter Marshall

The only people to get even with
are those who have helped us.

Unknown

When people are serving,
life is no longer meaningless.

John Gardner

To exist is to change,
to change is to mature,
to mature is to go on
creating oneself endlessly.

Henry Berson

ℰ

The world is good-natured to
people who are
good-natured.

William Makepeace Thackeray

Did you ever see the customers
in health-food stores?
They are pale, skinny people
who look half-dead.

In a steak house, you see
robust, ruddy people.
They're dying, of course,
but they look terrific.

Bill Cosby

Thousands of candles
can be lighted
from a single candle,
and the life of the candle will
not be shortened.

Buddha

Compassion for yourself translates
into compassion for others.

Suki Jay Munsell

ℬ

When someone is in trouble,
don't annoy him by asking if
there is anything you can do.
Think up something appropriate
and do it.

E.W. Hove

He is richest
who is content
with the least.

Socrates

The future is not a gift—
it is an achievement.

Harry Lauder

We have a limited number of heartbeats
and we're in charge of how we use them.

Peter Alsop

If you want others to be happy,
practice compassion.
If you want to be happy,
practice compassion.

The Dalai Lama

I will speak ill of no one,
and speak
all the good I know
of everyone.

Benjamin Franklin

What we think,
we become.

Buddha

The measure of life
is not its duration,
but its donation.

Peter Marshall

Real success is finding
your lifework in
the work that you love.

David McCullough

It matters not
how long we live,
but how.

Philip James Bailey

ᓂ

Keep away from people
who try to belittle your ambitions.
Small people always do that,
but the really great
make you feel that you, too,
can become great.

Mark Twain

One must never lose time
in vainly regretting the past
or in complaining against the changes
which cause us discomfort,
for change is the essence of life.

Anatole France

Friends are kind to each other's hopes.
They cherish each other's dreams.

Henry David Thoreau

Failure is the opportunity
to begin again more intelligently.

Anonymous

Surround yourself with people who
respect you and treat you well.

Claudia Black

ᖇ

Do not take life too seriously.
You will never get out of it alive.

Elbert Hubbard

Half an hour's meditation
each day is essential, except
when you are busy—
then a full hour is needed.

St. Francis de Sales

The great gift of family life
is to be intimately acquainted with people
you might never even have introduced yourself to
had life not done it for you.

Kendall Hailey

Try not to become a man of success,
but a man of value.

Albert Einstein

When all is said and done,
more is said than done.

Lou Holtz

A life is not important,
except in the impact it has
on other's lives.

Jackie Robinson

Faith in small things has repercussions that
ripple all the way out.
In a huge, dark room
a little match can light up the place.

Joni Eareckson Tada

Treasure this day,
and treasure yourself.
Truly, neither will ever happen again.

Ray Bradbury

The manner of giving
is worth more than the gift.

Pierre Corneille

I used to say,
"I sure hope things change."
Then I learned that
the only way things are going
to change for me is
when I change.

Unknown

You can't deny laughter.
When it comes,
it plops down in your favorite chair
and stays as long as it wants.

Stephen King

Creativity is
God's gift to you.

What you do with it
is your gift to God.

Bob Moawad

Though no one can go back and
make a brand new start, anyone
can start from now and
make a brand new ending.

Carl Bard

I will act as if
I do make a difference.

William James

People must believe in each other,
and feel that it can be done and must be done;
in that way they are enormously strong.

Vincent van Gogh

Surround yourself with people
who believe you can.

Dan Zadra

Our greatest weakness lies in giving up.
The most certain way to succeed
is to always try just one more time.

Thomas Edison

There are two theories to
arguing with women.

Neither one works.

Unknown

Retirement at sixty-five is ridiculous.
When I was sixty-five I still had pimples.

George Burns

Talents are best nurtured in solitude.
Character is best formed in
the stormy billows of the world.

Johann Wolfgang Von Goethe

When I hear the words of
God spoken through Jesus,
I listen carefully
and know they are
the TRUTH of our souls.

Charles Fillmore

The only thing that stands between
a man and what he wants from life
is often merely the will to try it and
the faith to believe that
it is possible.

Richard M. Devos

Take calculated risks.
That is quite different
from being rash.

George S. Patton

Character and personal force
are the only investments that
are worth anything.

Walt Whitman

Your own words are
the bricks and mortar
of the dreams you want
to realize.

Your words are
the greatest power you have.

The words you choose and their use
establish the life
you experience.

Sonia Croquette

The truth of the matter is that
you always know the right thing to do.

The hard part is doing it.

General Norman Schwarzkopf

What you are
will show
in what you do.

Thomas A. Edison

As you get older,
don't slow down.
Speedup.
There's still time left.

Malcolm Forbes

We shall never know
all the good that
a simple smile can do.

Mother Theresa

Happiness is not
a state to arrive at,
but a manner of traveling.

Margaret Lee Runbeck

We are what we repeatedly do.
Excellence, therefore, is not an act
but a habit.

Aristotle

Forgiveness is a gift you
give yourself.

Suzanne Somers

When you rise in the morning,
form a resolution to make the day
a happy one for a fellow creature.

Sydney Smith

Understand that
the right to choose
your own path
is a sacred privilege.

Use it.

Dwell in possibility.

Oprah Winfrey

Above all—
be the heroine of your own life,
not the victim.

Nora Ephron

Our lives improve only when
we take chances—
and the first and most difficult
risk we can take is
to be honest with ourselves.

Walter Anderson

If I have the belief that I can do it,
I shall surely acquire the capacity to do it.

Mahatma Gandhi

After thirty,
a body has a mind of its own.

Bette Midler

Most people see what is, and
never see what can be.

Albert Einstein

The secret of success in life
is for a man to be ready for
his opportunity when it comes.

Earl of Beaconsfield

Happy are those who dream dreams
and are ready to pay the price
to make them come true.

Leon J. Suenes

The talent of success
is nothing more than doing
what you can do, well.

Henry Longfellow

Kindness is never wasted.
If it has no effect on the recipient,
at least it benefits the bestower.

S. H. Simmons

If your success is not on your own terms,
if it looks good to the world
but does not feel good in your heart,
then it is not success at all.

Anna Quindlen

You will never change your life until
you change something you do daily.
The secret of your success
is found in your daily routine.

John C. Maxwell

*Every time you state
what you want or believe,
you're the first to hear it.*

*It's a message to you and others
about what you think is possible.*

Don't put a ceiling on yourself.

Oprah Winfrey

Show class,
have pride, and
display character.

If you do,
winning takes care of
itself.

Paul Bryant

The essential thing is not
knowledge,
but character.

Joseph Le Conte

What lies behind us
and what lies before us
are tiny matters compared to
what lies within us.

Ralph Waldo Emerson

I cannot give you the formula for success,
but I can give you the formula for failure—
try to please everybody.

Herbert Bayard Swope

Knowing is not enough;
we must apply.

Willing is not enough;
we must do.

Johann Wolfgang von Goethe

The higher your energy level,
the more efficient your body.

The more efficient your body,
the better you feel and
the more you will use your talent to
produce outstanding results.

Anthony Robbins

Angels fly because
they take themselves lightly.

Anonymous

Being defeated is often
a temporary condition.

Giving up is what
makes it permanent.

Marilyn Vos Savant

Finish each day
and be done with it.

You have done what you could;
some blunders and absurdities have crept in;
forget them as soon as you can.

Tomorrow is a new day;
you shall begin it serenely and
with too high a spirit
to be encumbered
with your old nonsense.

Ralph Waldo Emerson

Step by step.

I can't think of any other way
of accomplishing anything.

Michael Jordan

Never fear shadows.

They simply mean there's
a light shining somewhere nearby.

Ruth E. Renkel

He lives long who lives well;
and time misspent is not lived but lost.

Thomas Fuller

Worrying about something that
may never happen
is like paying interest on money
you may never borrow.

Unknown

The door of opportunity won't open
unless you do some pushing.

Anonymous

The most difficult thing
I have ever had to do
is follow the guidance
I prayed for.

Albert Schweitzer

The best way out
is always through.

Robert Frost

The only way to live
is to accept each minute as
an unrepeatable miracle,
which is exactly what it is:
a miracle and unrepeatable.

Storm Jameson

You gain strength,
courage and confidence by
every experience in which
you really stop to look fear in the face.

You are able to say to yourself,
"I lived through this horror.
I can take the next thing that comes along."

Eleanor Roosevelt

All the wonders you seek are
within yourself.

Sir Thomas Brown

Make up your mind to be happy.
Learn to find pleasure in simple things.

Robert Louis Stevenson

Meditate.
Live purely.
Be quiet.
Do your work with mastery.

Like the moon,
come out from behind the clouds.

Shine.

Buddha

Sacrifice is giving up something
good for something better.

Anonymous

Find ecstasy in life;
the mere sense of living is joy enough.

Emily Dickinson

Character is,
for the most part,
simply habit become fixed.

C. H. Parkhurst

In living,
choose your ground well.

In thought,
stay deep in the heart.

In relationship,
be generous.

In speaking,
hold to truth.

In leadership,
be organized.

In work,
do your best.

In action,
be timely.

The Tao Te Ching

No legacy is so rich as honesty.

William Shakespeare

I have no romantic feelings about age.
Either you are interesting at any age or
you are not.

There is nothing
particularly interesting about
being old—or being young—
for that matter.

Katharine Hepburn

୬

They always say
time changes things,
but you actually have to
change them yourself.

Andy Warhol

Life is not measured by
the number of breaths we take,
but by the moments that
take our breath away.

George Carlin

There is only one corner of the universe
you can be certain of improving
and that's your own self.

Aldous Huxley

If you tell the truth
you don't have to remember anything.

Mark Twain

I honor in YOU the Divine
that I honor within myself.
And I know we are one.

Dr. Deepak Chopra

୬

Grant me the courage not to give up
even though I think it's hopeless.

Chester W. Nimitz

All journeys have secret destinations of which
the traveler is unaware.

Martin Buber

My advice to you is
not to inquire why or whither,
but just to enjoy your ice cream
while it's on your plate.

Thornton Wilder

Be yourself.
No one can ever tell you
you're doing it wrong.

James Leo Herlihy

Most of the important things in the world
have been accomplished by people
who have kept on trying when there
seemed to be no hope at all.

Dale Carnegie

A generous heart, kind speech,
and a life of service and compassion
are the things which renew humanity.

Buddha

To be courageous means to be afraid
but to go a little step forward anyway.

Beverly Smith

I celebrate myself, and
sing myself.

Walt Whitman

Do what you can,
with what you have,
where you are.

Theodore Roosevelt

Health is the greatest gift,
contentment the greatest wealth,
faithfulness the best relationship.

Buddha

Every artist was first
an amateur.

Ralph Waldo Emerson

Be kinder than necessary, for
everyone you meet
is fighting some kind of battle.

Unknown

Man's mind,
once stretched by a new idea,
never regains its original dimensions.

Oliver Wendell Holmes, Jr.

To face despair
and not give in to it,
that's courage.

Ted Koppel

Life may not be
the party we hoped for . . .
but while we are here
we might as well dance.

Unknown

If you can imagine it,
you can achieve it;
if you can dream it,
you can become it.

William Arthur Ward

It is the heart that makes a man rich.
He is rich according to what he is,
not according to what he has.

Henry Ward Beecher

First keep the peace within yourself,
then you can also bring peace to others.

Thomas Kempis

Happiness depends
upon ourselves.

Aristotle

The way we look
is the outer expression
of how we feel in side.

Unknown

If the only prayer
you say in your whole life is,
"Thank you"—
that would suffice.

Meister Eckhart

All progress occurs
because people dare
to be different.

Harry Milner

I decided long ago never to look at
the right side of the menu
or the price tags on clothes—

otherwise I would have starved, naked.

Helen Hayes

It may be that those
who do most,
dream most.

Stephen Leacock

Happiness is not achieved by
the conscious pursuit of happiness;
it is generally the by-product
of other activities.

Aldous Huxley

You can't help getting older, but
you don't have to get old.

George Burns

When you reach for the stars,
you may not get one,
but then you won't come up
with a handful of mud, either.

So never be afraid to
reach for them
no matter what.

Leo Burnett

There are those
who give with joy, and
that joy is their reward.

Kahlil Gibran

Practice doesn't always make perfect;
perfect practice makes perfect.

Vincent Lombardi

Keep your fears to yourself.
Share your courage with others.

Robert Louis Stevenson

Joy can be real only if people look
on their life as a service, and
have a definite object in life
outside themselves and
their personal happiness.

Leo Nikolaevich Tolstoy

I can feel guilty about the past,
apprehensive about the future,
but only in the present can I act.

The ability to be in the present moment is
a major component of mental wellness.

Abraham Maslow

If there is no struggle,
there is no progress.

Frederick Douglass

We should be too big to take offense
and too noble to give it.

Abraham Lincoln

To carry a grudge is like being
stung to death by one bee.

William H. Walton

What a lovely surprise to finally discover
how un-lonely being alone can be.

Ellen Burstyn

Believe you can
and you are half way there.

Theodore Roosevelt

The person who tries to live alone
will not succeed as a human being.
His heart withers if it does not
answer another heart.

His mind shrinks away if he hears only
the echoes of his own thoughts and
finds no other inspiration.

Pearl S. Buck

Since you get more joy out of
giving joy to others,
you should put a good deal of thought
into the happiness that you are able to give.

Eleanor Roosevelt

Dost thou love life?

Then do not squander time,
for that's the stuff life is made of.

Benjamin Franklin

Life is a great big canvas,
and you should throw
all the paint on it you can.

Danny Kaye

Even if you're on the right track,
you'll get run over if you just sit there.

Will Rogers

Today is
yesterday's pupil.

Thomas Fuller

Thirty-five is when
you finally get your head together and then
your body starts to fall apart.

Caryn Leschen

Life isn't about finding yourself.
Life is about creating yourself.

George Shaw

When all is said and done,
the only change that will make a difference
is the transformation of the human heart.

Peter Senge

We can throw stones,
complain about them,
stumble on them,
climb over them,
or build with them.

William Arthur Ward

You can tell more about a person by
what he says about others than you can by
what others say about him.

Anonymous

You're happiest while you're
making the greatest contribution.

Robert F. Kennedy

We only learn our limits
by going beyond them.

Unknown

More bad news for pessimists—
optimists live longer

Unknown

Bravery is believing in yourself,
and that is something no one else
can teach you.

El Cordobes

Home is where they
understand you.

Christian Morgenstern

Service is the rent we pay to be living.

It is the very purpose of life and
not something you do
in your spare time.

Marian Wright Edellman

Great opportunities to help others
seldom come, but
small ones surround us
every day.

Sally Koch

There are two ways of meeting difficulties;
you alter the difficulties,
or you alter yourself to meet them

Phyllis Battome

You are here to enable
the divine purpose of
the universe to unfold.
That is how important you are.

Eckhart Tolle

Once I got a fortune cookie that said,
"To remember is to understand."

Unknown

A good judge remembers what it was like
to be a lawyer.

A good boss remembers what it was like
to be an employee.

A good parent remembers what it was like
to be a child.

Anna Quindlen

The most important thing in communication is
to hear what isn't being said.

Peter Drucker

If we are to have real peace,
we must begin with the children.

Mahatma Gandhi

There is only one person
who could ever make you happy,
and that person is you.

David Burns

If there's one thing tougher
than being a teenager—
it's having one.

Gordon McLean

A man who dares waste
one hour of time
has not discovered the
value of life.

Charles Darwin

Challenges are what make
life interesting;
overcoming them is what makes
life meaningful.

Joshua J. Marine

If you have no goal other than
personal happiness,
you'll never achieve it.

If you want to be happy,
pursue something vigorously and
happiness will catch up with you.

Ed Diener

You are always with yourself so
you might as well enjoy the company.

Diane Von Furstenberg